GW01326133

For My Mother

Introduction

For the past 20 years I have kept a diary. In the early days the entries were written in a great hurry, often late at night and frequently spoke of the angst, pain and suffering I seemed to experience as a young teenager.

For many years I only ever wrote in the diary when there was some kind of painful emotion I felt the need to express privately or some kind of crisis in my life that I wanted to find a solution to. There was always a sense of trying to escape from the drama of life and the longing I felt to be free from suffering is very apparent in my early journals.

Although there have been some periods in the last 20 years when I've not written the diary, I have returned to the practice again and again. In recent years I've written in the diary daily.

In my late twenties I was diagnosed with a life threatening illness and this sparked off an intense spiritual search. Faced with the possibility of death, I suddenly got very busy trying to find out why I was here, where I'd come from, what happens when we die and so on.

This led me to many teachings, writings and practices that in the end were all about improving this thing called my life. Eventually,

I decided that enlightenment was what I wanted, believing the stories that it could happen to me and that I could be beyond suffering.

Like most people, prior to spiritual seeking I'd been looking for fulfilment and satisfaction in life. I tended to focus mostly on work, following my dream of becoming an actor. I truly believed that I'd be happy once I'd achieved my ambitions.

I managed to get into a very good drama school in London and for a number of years worked professionally as an actor. The reality of a life in the theatre however did not live up to the dreams I'd had in my youth and I soon began looking elsewhere for fulfilment.

Again, like many people, I turned to the same tools of seeking in the spiritual search, looking always to complete myself, to become whole again. It was not until I came across the teachings of nonduality and the various different expressions of various different teachers did I finally contemplate the suggestion that promised to bring the whole seeking game to a tremendous, collapsing end.

This suggestion is expressed through the writings collected here. Through early blog posts and extracts from my private journals the unfolding of this awesome suggestion can be seen.

It is the gentle and fearless suggestion that what is so desperately sought after is already happening. That we already are what we seek, that nothing was ever lost and that we never left the home we so deeply long for.

5th July 2010

Nothing appears to speak. Appears to write. Nothing enjoys being everything, it seems.

We cannot even say that you are nothing. Or that I am nothing. For who is there to be nothing? There is no one. This is truly liberating.

If there is no one, then who gets upset? Who gets angry, or sad? Anger can arise, does arise. Sadness arises. It arises for no one. And when there is no one holding onto it, when there is no one creating a story around it, anger or sadness seems to spin out into nothing soon enough.

16th July 2010

Me has woken up. It's as if being, simply being is an empty room and now the self has stormed back in, demanding to know what's been going on in its absence. It kicks over the tables and the chairs, causes a right commotion and stands, hands on hips asking "What the hell has been going on?"

There is no me in there of course. It's just a story. Being arises as me, the appearance of me in the room is the emptiness appearing as that. Me wants to have being, to do being. Being can't be had or done though. It doesn't belong to anyone.

The experience of being a separate individual seems so very real. What the individual feels, sees, hears and thinks feels at times like it's the only reality. And yet there is now a kind of spaciousness that is there, an awareness if you like of the fleetingness of this individual. Awakening is happening and suddenly there can be a clear moment of no one there but aliveness is still happening, life is still happening, this is still this.

It's seen then that there is no death. Being is already everything, including the individual. It's also seen that there is no free will, no choice. I don't choose this or that, it simply happens. I am being lived. Being is living as the body mind, as the appearance of the individual, as this pain or this constriction or this story. I don't own anything, I don't have anything. This is total emptiness where the fullness of life is simply lived, not kept or owned.

27th July 2010

This is not interesting. The individual wants there to be something. Can only see 'something'. When there is only the individual (or the 'self', or 'ego') it wants something tangible that it can grasp and hang onto.

There is nothing here for the individual. Except the possibility of its death. And yet, the individual hears that its own death might bring it 'something' and so it wants that too. It's quite amusing.

When this was first seen it did seem that an awakening happened. There was a sudden sense of ease, of wonder. I remember feeling laughter bubble up inside of me. I then wanted to have that experience, to bottle it and keep it for myself. I never had anything in the first place. I had disappeared. And then I came back and from my individual perspective, decided that something important had happened and wanted it to happen again. My wanting it, my seeking of it prevented the finding of it. How can I find what is already here? It's like looking for your glasses when they sit on your face.

I can't find what has never been lost. Finding something means that a search begins. But the search just takes me further away from the perceived goal. I go out into the world, looking all over for my heart's desire. I travel to distant places, listen to different teachers, buy this book and that book, study and learn only to return home, exhausted by the search. And then I realise that what I was looking for was with me all along. In fact, it's not even with 'me'. I am it. I never had to go anywhere or do anything.

So, the individual seeks. It attempts to score itself a good deal. It wants this or that, so that it can feel this or that. It might want money or fame, power or influence. It might want to be a victim. It might want to no longer be. There is an underlying sensation of 'not enough' in separation. There's a hole that needs filling. And that fuels the seeking, fuels the search. It's a sense of lack, almost like hunger or craving.

That sense of perceived lack, that hunger powers the search. It doesn't really matter what it searches for. Some people find some of things they were searching for, like money or sex, or power or a relationship and after a while the self gets hungry again. That wasn't it. There must be something else.

And when the individual hears about this thing called 'enlightenment' it thinks that must be a prize worth having. This is the real deal. This will be the final search. And it turns it's power of manipulation and negotiation to the spiritual search. There must be something I can do, steps I can take.

There is nothing that needs to be done. Being can't be done.

2nd August 2010

I feel dreadful. Longing has returned. I feel the need to do something amazing, something meaningful. What is that about? The need to be important? The need to be special? Wish I could settle on something. I feel locked into the thought that I should be doing something worthwhile, that I should be helping in some way but I don't know what or how.

Something is calling me but I can't hear what it is saying or even tell what it is. I keep feeling like something massive is happening, the falling away of self or some kind of awakening and then all of a sudden the old feelings of boredom or restlessness return. I don't understand. I just want to be free. And yet I can see so clearly that the whole time I am there demanding to be free, there is the prison of the person. I'm trapped in this 'me' cycle. One moment I'm there, the next there is just space, just emptiness, just the unfolding of this moment.

10th August 2010

The experience of being a separate individual is very powerful and at times, all encompassing. When there is a 'me' there is usually suffering. The suffering can of course be very subtle. The slight ache of wanting. Or suffering can be so intense that the individual craves its own demise.

The problem for the individual is that it cannot confront its own absence. It's impossible. For there to be any kind of confrontation, I have to approach my own absence and for me to approach anything I have to be there. It's a futile activity.

Freedom is the absence of the individual. Liberation or enlightenment is the loss of self. Total loss. It is the death of 'me' while the body/mind continues to arise.

Wholeness is inevitable. We return to wholeness while incarnated in body and mind or we return to wholeness when the body/mind dies. Either way, the death of the individual has occurred.

The experience of being separate seems very real. The 5 senses (and also the experience of emotions and thought) seem to confirm that I'm in here and everything else is out there. As far as the individual is concerned, it is not connected to anything that it can see or sense as separate from itself. And it sees pretty much everything that's not 'me' as something other.

Separation gives rise to seeking. This is because in separation, there is a perception of lack. The individual feels as if it has lost something and needs to find it. Seeking takes myriad forms. Some of them very obvious and gross and some quite subtle. All seeking is ultimately the seeking to return to wholeness. The individual interprets that goal as something that will cure the pain the individual may be experiencing. And so the seeking of it can intensify. And as the seeking intensifies, so the separation from wholeness grows.

When the individual hears this, it might think that it needs to stop seeking. Yet this is another layer of seeking. I seek to end seeking. I want to not want. But of course, wanting to not want is just more wanting. Is just more seeking.

'What do I do then?' cries the self!

The individual, the self, the ego (call it what you will) is always looking for what it can do. It is more of its wanting, of its seeking. It wants a process, it wants to take steps that will bring it to its destination. When actually, the step you are taking now is the destination. This is it. Whatever is happening. Writing words on a computer, reading words on a screen, thoughts arising, sitting on a chair, confusion, frustration, anger, desperation… it's all included in what is. And what is, is what's happening.

19th August 2010

So, what is there to say? What is there to do? My wanting liberation keeps it away. It is never fully kept away of course because even the appearance of something that thinks it is kept away, is being, being that. Being is all there is and so can't be kept away. I can only tell that story and yet it can be seen that even the telling of the story is freedom dressing up as that.

Confusion about it, is it. Seeking for it, is it. Oneness arising as a separate individual looking for oneness IS oneness doing and being that. I cannot know what this is. This sadness, this boredom, this feeling of restlessness. In truth it is a mystery. Before I call it sadness, before I call it boredom or restlessness, it is simply a form appearing in emptiness. It is another wonder of life. It's all life energy, all the one consciousness in a million different disguises.

It is this weight in the body, this humidity. A heaviness, a tightness. And the story about the heaviness, where it came from, where it's going, why it's here and what I think I can do about it.

No purpose. Why does the rain fall? It needs no purpose.

29th August 2010

What does nothing say? For nothing to say anything, there must be something. And that's okay. Because nothing is everything. So, nothing says this.

What does nothing do? Nothing does this. Or that.

The separate individual (that is you or I) wants answers. Wants steps it can take to reach enlightenment. To make liberation happen. To escape our fear, our pain, our past. Or to create bliss, joy, our future. In that seeking to avoid pain and create pleasure, the simplicity of 'just this' is overlooked. What we are seeking is happening now. The source of the seeking is what is sought.

These words can only be concepts or pointers. These words can only be something arising out of nothing. The fascinating thing about simply being is that it seems to delight in delivering this message. It seems to delight in everything, in fact. This computer screen, the tap tap of the keys, the thoughts arising now. There is total delight in that.

What can you do to find that? Absolutely nothing at all. You can't find it because it is the absence of you. The idea of you (or me) or an individual self is nothing more than the thought of me and what is mine. That 'me' thought, the idea of me gives rise to suffering. Because along with the thought of me is the belief that I am separate. I am in here and you or that or life is out there. The result of that belief that I am separate is a very real sense of lack, of need. The individual and separate self is in a constant state of 'not enough'. And so it goes out into this seemingly separate world and looks for things, experiences, thoughts, feelings to make itself feel whole. To make itself feel better. To heal this wound.

The separate me, the separate self is wounded. It believes that it lost something. That loss is felt in the body as emotion. And to compensate for the loss it seeks in the world of form for things it thinks it wants. So, you are looking for something you think you want. You might think you want ice cream, or sex or a better relationship or happiness or freedom from addiction or freedom from sadness, from pain, from anger, from doubt. You might think you want enlightenment, yes that will fix me. What you're really looking for is a way home. A way to find what you think has been lost.

But it never went anywhere. What you're looking for is right here. The problem is, it can't be seen by the mind. It can't be identified. You can't buy it, you can't work for it, you can't attain it. Because it already is this. The hopeless searching already is this, being that. Being searching.

Some people call this non-duality, or say that what is being pointed to here is 'being' or 'presence'. But the problem that arises when we speak of it this way is that the mind or the individual or you get hold of that word and create a concept out of it and believe that because it seems that it can be named, then it has now been identified and therefore there must be steps I can take to get it. Get it and keep it. And do something with it.

What do you do with being, the individual asks, the mind asks. What's it for? What's it do? How do I operate it? Being can't be done. How can you do something you are?

2nd September 2010

Sat at my desk drinking red wine in my lovely little flat. I'm so lucky.

More and more there is a pull towards talking about awakening, communicating what cannot be communicated, what cannot be expressed in words. And yet, the words too are glorious being, being words about being.

The sun is pouring through the bedroom window as it does in the late afternoon. My neighbour is out with his mower cutting the grass and I sit at my desk writing. I seem to be dancing in and out of being at the moment. One day there is the empty is-ness of just this happening, the next day there is the return of the separate self making demands of being, creating havoc. The energy of wanting, of yearning and longing suddenly re-emerges from the shadows, catching me off guard and running amok. And somewhere in amongst the mess I sit and wonder if this will ever be over, wonder if life will always be like this.

Is it ego that desires to be a mouthpiece for this message? Or is it the simple joy in talking about this that fuels the desire to reach out? A desire to escape the prison of the mundane perhaps, or a need to stand out and be special?

I do not know. All I know is that things will never be the same again, despite my fears that longing will continue to irritate. There continue to be a series of explosions where the structure and edifice of separation is damaged, the foundations rupturing and the building coming down.

9th September 2010

There is only being. And what arises in being, is the belief that I am an individual that is separate from being. And out of that separation comes a deep sense of loss, which inspires seeking and searching for something to fill the hole felt by the perceived loss.

It is felt that something is missing. And for most people, a search in the world of form takes place. We seek to have better relationships, better places to live, more money, more fun, more excitement, better holidays, better and better experiences. And for some people, that worldly seeking is found to be never ending. As soon as one thing is found, the search for something new begins. And then, for some begins the spiritual search.

The problem with the spiritual search is that we employ the very same tactics that we used in the worldly search. In fact, the real problem with the spiritual search is the seeking itself. Because, what is sought is found to already be here when seeking stops. Liberation from the pain of separation, freedom from that deep sense of loss and freedom from the never ending list of desires only comes when it is seen there is no one and therefore no need to search.

This message is radical. There is no need to search! What you are looking for never went away. It never came and it never went away.

The individual hears this and thinks it has found a precious clue. It hears this and thinks that it can simply call off the search, stop seeking and then liberation will be the prize. But there is no one to receive the prize. The fundamental shift in perception after liberation is the seeing that there is no one. There is no self. Who sees that? No one sees that. It is seen. You could say that being sees that all there is, is being. Being sees that there is no individual.

So, if there is no individual who is going to stop seeking? Who's going to call off the search?

14th September 2010

The simple wonder of what is seems to have no end. What is happening is always enough. Just sounds, smells, thoughts, feelings, sensations in the body. A symphony. Pen moving across page. There is sheer delight in just that. Utter peace. The war is over. No more wrangling, no more conflict... just this... glorious this.

24th September 2010

All there is, is this. All there is, is being. Being, being this.

And what arises in that is the belief and experience of being a separate individual. I am me and things happen to me. I have a life and it's my job to make that life work. And what arises out of that sense of separation is a sometimes subtle and sometimes overwhelming sense of loss, dissatisfaction and lack.

That then gives rise to seeking. The individual seeks to fill the sense of lack. It may fill it with money, power, sex, drugs, food, anything really that the person endows with the belief that the getting of it will fill that ever present sense of lack.

The individual may find what it thinks it's looking for and for a time may experience some kind of relief or abatement of the nagging need for more. Or the nagging sensation that this is not it.

Soon enough however, any feeling of pleasure or satisfaction with what is found is realised to be temporary. The good feeling of getting what one thinks one wants soon fades. And the search is picked up again. This happens with the spiritual search as much with any other kind of seeking.

And so the search goes on. We look for things we can do, have or be to dispel the disquiet that accompanies the sense of being a separate individual. The problem is not that me can't get what it wants. Often it can. The problem is me. The problem is that we think we are separate individuals when actually we are not.

All there is, is being. Being is appearing as a separate individual looking for itself. There is nothing that is not being.

30th September 2010

The separate self is in perpetual motion. It is movement. Not only is it seeking something outside itself, but it is the search also.

This evening I can feel movement within. I can feel the pull of need, the pull of desire. I'm aware though that nothing in this world can satisfy that desire. The only thing that will satisfy is not a thing at all. And it's already happening.

It's this. Life itself. There is no need to desire it because I am it. It is already happening.

3rd October 2010

The individual does not get the greatest joke. The cosmic joke. It does not find it funny. Being is a comedian with an audience that never laughs.

The individual (the self, you, me) cannot even hear the joke.

The individual hears that there is this great party. It's a party called enlightenment, and it's heard that it is possible to get an invite. So, it goes hunting the known world for an invite. It might learn that it needs to meditate for 20 years and then it will be invited to the party. So, off it goes and sits on a cushion for 20 years. But still there is no invite to the party.

The joke is, the party does not start until there is no individual. As soon as there is no individual, then the party starts. So, the individual hears this and thinks: Right, I'll just get rid of myself then. Then I can go to the party!

But no one can go the party. It's the greatest party on earth and there's no one there, having an amazing time!

When the individual ceases to hunt down the invite and then ceases to be all together, then the party apparently starts. And it's thrilling, for no one. Which is a great tragedy for the individual even though that is what it thinks it wants.

7th October 2010

I can look inside and see what is arising. That does seem to help. To be present with what is. It's a kind of process I guess, because there is someone there doing it, someone trying to be present with what is. There is what is and then me trying to be with it!

When there is no individual, when there is no one looking there is no one to become present. There already is presence. Presence is what all this happens in.

I used to have so many different practices. So many plans to fix this broken me. To see that it comes and goes with such regularity is shocking and seems to confirm it's unreality. The solidity of this entity called me is loosening, it's crumbling away leaving such a resounding and profound peace that it is startling.

24th October 2010

The message of non-duality is frustrating for the individual. It can't really hear this message because the message points to the absence of the individual and the individual cannot be present at its own death.

So, often the message is simply rejected because it's being heard by the individual and the last thing the individual wants is to not be. Or, the message is heard by an individual who wants what it thinks the message is pointing to. The message is actually pointing to the absence of the individual but that does not stop some individuals wanting that. The seeker can want to stop seeking. But the only way it knows to get it is to seek for it. In fact, in the world of the seeker there is lots of getting, lots of possessing and usually a journey.

One of the most frustrating things for the seeker is the revelation that there are no steps. You cannot approach being. There are no steps towards it. And so, the individual seeker hears this and throws it's hands up in the air in desperation, asking "Well, what is the point if I can't get there?"

The message of non-duality is saying that there is no 'there' to get to. What is being suggested is that you are already where you want so desperately to be. In fact, you are not 'there' as such. It is clearer to say that what you want is the simplicity of timeless being, and that being is already being. You are that being. This is it. It's only seen as not it when you're out there looking for it.

As seekers, we believe that liberation, or Being or enlightenment is some state that we can reach and therefore we deduce that there are steps we can take to enter such a state. States however are always passing. They come and go. They come and go within Being. Being is the one constant. It is where all states come and go. It is nothing and everything. It is the state of bliss and it is the state of frustration.

The message of non-duality, clearly and compassionately communicated will lovingly destroy all illusion. The illusion here is that if I take certain action steps they will lead me from A – B. You can sate hunger by eating a meal, so you reasonably conclude that there are also steps to take to bring about liberation. This message says that there are no steps to get you 'there' because you are there already. Any steps you take will simply take you away from here.

And yet… even that is not the truth. Because the steps themselves are still this. Whatever is happening is being. And if steps towards or steps away are happening, then that is being also. They don't lead anywhere though. The steps themselves are liberation. The belief that they lead somewhere is the illusion. So, in that sense there are no steps.

Each step is being, is freedom.

1ˢᵗ November 2010

The day has spiralled into blank boredom and misery. A feeling of utter blankness has returned. It's like the world is seen from within a thick glass box. Nothing has any joy in it today. There is no pleasure anywhere. No process will ever work, no steps will ever take you where you want to be.

It's a kind of despair.

What is happening is a waiting. Waiting for the moment of liberation, waiting for some kind of event. Waiting for the sense of being an individual to collapse, waiting for me to drop away, for the end of separation.

The problem in this waiting is that the individual is doing it. I am doing waiting. The individual continues, the dream of separation goes on.

7th November 2010

It's here. In the movement of the pen across the page. I can't always see it, but it's here. Here in the beating of the heart, in the pain of emotion, in the movement of wanting, in the feeling of worthlessness. It's in the feeling of boredom, the sound of the traffic, the flickering of thoughts.

The individual thinks that everything must be resolved before this is seen, before freedom can simply be. It believes that all of its demands for a better me must be met first. It cannot see that freedom is freely being that, being the desire, the demands, the seeking, the longing.

18th November 2010

Being is being everything already. It is being these words on a screen. It is being this, whatever this is right now. Being is also appearing as an individual. As 'me' or 'you'. That 'me' becomes a seemingly solid entity that then feels separate from everything else. Separate from Being. Yet, it is Being. Being is dreaming that it is separate.

In believing itself to be separate from Being, the individual experiences a sense of loss, of lack, of pain. Something is missing. The individual feels itself to be alone, it is homesick. So, we go out into the world and look for something to complete 'me'.

This individual (which is simply Being, being and individual) begins to seek Being. It can never find it however, because it already is what it seeks. This is the great cosmic joke. Laughter spills forth when this is seen.

In the dream, everything is always changing. Sometimes the dream is a good dream. Sometimes it is a nightmare. And sometimes, the dreamer knows it is dreaming and wants to wake up. But the dreamer can only dream. If it did not dream, it would not be a dreamer. It can only dream.

Yet, Being is the dream also. Being is dreaming. The dream is not apart from Being. So, if awakening happens no one wakes up. The dreamer is simply no more. It vanishes.

22nd November 2010

Have come out to the local pub for a change of scene. I feel like I've been going at quite a speed today, a fast internal rhythm.

The feeling of oneness keeps fading in and out. The individual returns quite fast at times and thinks that oneness means feeling calm, spacious, light and airy. It thinks oneness is only the nice feelings of relaxation, the free floating feelings of peace and love.

Oneness of course includes everything. It includes the depression or the blankness, the panic and the anxiety. It is all colours. Paradoxically, when the emptiness in which panic or blankness happens is felt, is seen.. then a subtle kind of joy emanates, even in the experience of suffering.

29th November 2010

Liberation cannot be known. It cannot be known, because it's just being. There is no knowing in it's being and it's not happening to anyone.

If there are no people and the clouds move across the sky, it is not known. It is just happening. There is no one there to know it. It is simply happening.

That is what we are. We are simply the being that happens.

You leave your home in the morning and return to find a pipe has burst and flooded your house. When you were at work and the pipe first broke and the water began to leak into the rooms in the house, it was not yet known. It was simply happening. It just was, pipe bursting, water flowing… just being, being that.

And then you come home and you now know what has happened. There is a knower, knowing what it thinks is the known. The pipe has burst and caused a flood. You think you know what happened and what is happening.

All that is happening, is being, being. You are not a you, you are that being. Being does not know. Being is.

You are that being. Not 'a' being. You are the being. You, are being. This, is being. You are not a you, you are happening. You are not an happening, you are not happening to anyone or anything, you are happening itself. You are being, happening. You are the being, you are the happening.

Being is happening. Being is what happens, and being is what happened. Being, is nothing. Nothing, is happening.

Rejoice! It's a miracle! Nothing, is happening… You won't rejoice of course. But nothing will.

4th December 2010

It seems like being is always coming and going. Such a whirling dance. But being is the only constant. Being never comes and goes, it is the separate sense of self the disappears and then returns.

Me is a fleeting phenomenon, it comes and goes all the time. As does everything it claims to own. Feelings, states of mind, objects, stories. It's all shimmering in the light and half light.

Feel very restless. There is a sense of emptiness in my stomach, a feeling of irritation throughout the body. It's quite powerful. Maybe I should just got to bed?

8th December 2010

The separate sense of self, the individual (that is, you or me) continually seeks to appropriate liberation for itself. It wants a claim to fame and uses all the allure of promises of specialness that are so attractive to one who feels so desperately incomplete.

But when this is seen just as it is, the longings of the ego or the separate sense of self simply fall away. If they arise again, they arise. But no one is listening anymore and so those old tricks lose their power. No one is astonished, or wowed by the sleight of hand the individual once performed with such flair. It's insatiable drive for importance and grandeur dissolves in the immediacy of this.

In the wings, the individual is eavesdropping. It hears this message and makes a bid to dissolve itself more quickly, more permanently in order to have this prize.

The prize cannot be given and cannot be had or owned, known or kept. In reality, it is seen there is no prize. The prize is simply this. You never had to win it, it is always freely this. In that sense, it is a gift not a prize. But not a gift anyone can receive. It is the gift you are. Life is the gift.

14th December 2010

Sat in a cafe in the square. Felt the need to get out of the flat for a bit. Need to do some shopping and also just want to write somewhere different.

You can't escape freedom. There is nothing else but freedom. Even the appearance of this coffee shop, the pen, the feelings in the body, the thoughts of wanting freedom are all freedom being that.

And constantly the self wants something to do. "How can I get being, what can I do to have it?" Not seeing that there is only being, there is only this freedom dancing as everything.

19th December 2010

"It doesn't hide behind the bush, it is the bush"
Tony Parsons

It appears hidden. It doesn't hide behind everything, it hides as everything. It not concealing itself anywhere, it's revealing itself everywhere. It is everything. And it is everything happening. It is being, being everything happening. Being, is not a thing. It is nothing. Therefore, being is nothing and everything, happening. Here, now. There is no here and now really, it is just nothing and everything, happening.

It's not even happening here. It's nothing happening, nowhere! Nothing and everything, happening nowhere and everywhere.

21st December 2010

I feel very tired lately. Seem to need a lot of sleep.

This is totally fresh, totally new. It's never happened before and will never happen again. It's utter new-ness, utter freshness. Totally complete. The birds, the music, the pen, the ink, the coffee, the aliveness!

Totally free. Totally this. This sitting, this breathing, this blood, this body, these thoughts, these sensations. Suddenly, this is enough. This is already complete as it is. It was always like this. Always.

23rd December 2010

Enlightenment is not a state to be reached. The word enlightenment suggests some kind of event that takes place in time or a stage of development, evolution or even transcended state that rises above and includes all other states.

There is no final destination. The word enlightenment suggests there is something finite to achieve. It suggests some kind of arrival point is reached. It is not. This is a myth.

There is no such thing as enlightenment. Certainly not in the way it is commonly understood. Enlightenment is not a personal achievement. Has nothing to do at all with a person, you or me.

Enlightenment could be another word for being. All there is, is being. Being is nothing appearing as everything. Being simply is. Being is what is happening and all there is, is what's happening.

In that sense, being is the emptiness in which all other states appear and disappear. There is no such thing as a permanent state. All states of mind, emotional states and spiritual states are transient, are passing. This is what all passing states arise in and dissolve into. That, is timeless being.

Therefore, that cannot be reached or achieved. It can only be. When there is no longer a centre called 'me' it is seen that what is left, is being. Being simply being this.

28th December 2010

How long will this dance of self and no self go on for? Some people say it can go on forever... or at least until the body/mind dies. Ha! Of course, this entity called me dies each time there is no self, so death is happening frequently at the moment. The self dies and then is re-born, runs about a bit, creates a bit of chaos and then dies again leaving the peace of just this, just life unfolding.

When there is no self running about and demanding this or that, what unfolds can be stormy or forceful. All that is left if what is happening and that might be anger or running to catch a bus or hammering a nail into the wall or rushing to meet a deadline or loud music or debating politics. There simply is that with no me doing it, no me that it happens to.

And then time seems to pass and me returns with a story of how I've got to wake up, I've got to become liberated, I've got to benefit from this somehow. The irony is that when awakening happens, no one wakes up. When liberation happens it's seen that nothing happened at all. The end of separation is the end of an illusion so it is only the end of something that was appearing to be, the end of a deception. It's the end of something that was never happening.

6th January 2011

Being is paradoxical. It will never make sense to the mind. It cannot, in that sense, be understood. Yet it can be seen.

When the sense of being a separate self falls away, it is mildly surprising to see that nothing really changes. Life is still life, much the way it was before. And yet, everything changes.

One example of this, is the appearance of emotions and thoughts. Many people believe and some people teach that enlightenment is the absence of thought and one of its many rewards the absence of so called negative emotions.

When there is no individual, when it is seen that there is no 'me' in there, emotions and thoughts can still happen. But they are no longer happening to anyone. If thoughts arise, it is seen that no one is thinking them. And if emotions arise, it is seen that they are happening to no one.

Boredom comes. But because there is no one who is bored, boredom is then just something that is happening. It appears more like a physical sensation, much like an inconsequential ache or pain and is allowed to simply be. Because there is no bored person, no one wants to escape boredom.

It is the same with anger or sadness, irritation or fear. These emotions may arise but they do not happen to anyone. Nothing is held onto, including so called positive emotions. Delight may arise or excitement or passion. These too are allowed to be. No one is delighted, no one is exited. There is delight, there is excitement for no one.

The blank void that the individual fears results from its own absence is not, after all, the dreaded blank void. The miracle is that life goes on with or without you. It is noticed that life unfolds with infinitely more ease when there is no one that life happens to. But that is not a benefit for the individual, because of course there is no longer any individual that has a life. There is just life happening.

8th January 2011

Feeling quite anxious today. For the past few days I've not been able to recall any dreams and then this morning remembered a snippet of a dream I was having just before waking up. In it I was standing on stage talking and at the same time I was in the audience listening. I then also became aware that I was dreaming and started to write a blog post in my dream and then I woke up.

Then I started to feel this anxiety. Doesn't seem to be attached to anything in particular. I can't find a story about it. I have no idea where it's come from.

The day is unfolding. The clouds move across the sky, the air is crisp and cold. Anxiety flutters inside and then there is calm. My head is in the tigers mouth it seems and now I'm just waiting for it to be bitten off. There is nothing I can do and even doing nothing feels like some kind of strategy.

The me is always concerned with strategy. Give me something to do, let me work out some kind of plan so I can get somewhere better than here.

There is nowhere other than here. Here is all there is. This kitchen, this sofa, this pen, this anxiety, the clouds and the cold air.

13th January 2011

Individuals are driven to negotiate, manipulate and seek for what they want. Survival seems to be the name of the game. And if an individual is lucky enough to have some basic survival needs met then the game becomes more complex so that we can survive in more pleasant and comfortable surroundings.

There is nothing wrong with this of course, it's just what happens. As Richard Sylvester says, if you are in a prison it's intelligent to make that prison more comfortable.

We get a sense however that our desires for more or less of one thing or another is not quite it. It's too complicated. There are too many conditions. It is sensed that liberation is much simpler that all the striving to thrive. It is simpler even than arriving. Being is so utterly this and so utterly free that the instant we feel tempted to say that it is closer than our breath, or that it has any distinct qualities or that it provides any benefit, it is known that already we have caged it.

Being is everything. Separation cannot see everything however. In separation, from the perspective of I (or any perspective for that matter) everything is divided into millions of parts. Wholeness is not the opposite of separation. That is just more separation. Wholeness cannot ever be described. It simply is.

15th January 2011

It's been an odd day. Can't remember much of it. I phoned the hospital to tell them I cannot make the appointment they've given me. Took ages to get through. Then I went into town for a coffee and read the paper. Also began part of a blog post. But for most of the day I sort of feel like I've been dreaming or like I've been watching myself from the outside.

While I was reading the paper in the cafe, I caught sight of my arm and it didn't look like my arm. It was like I was outside of my body, looking at my arm. I don't recall any particular emotion that accompanied it.

On the way home in the car I had the strong feeling that I was not travelling any distance at all. That actually nothing ever moves anywhere, that nothing at all is happening. It came with a strong sense that there is no time and no space.

21st January 2011

My life is complicated. So is yours. Every life is complicated. But this is so totally simple. Since I started this blog, my life has taken numerous twists and turns. There has been much drama. And it's all about what is happening to me. At the centre of this drama is the character called me. I own so many things. My emotions, my fears, my crazy mind, my intense desires, often thwarted. My life. And it's my job to make it work.

And yet… being is all that is happening. Being is all that I am. Being is gloriously simple. It is being the story of me, it is being me having a drama. It is being the me that wants to simply be. It is being the strategising for peace, the desperate cry for freedom. The whole time this dance of seeking and searching goes on, being quietly, constantly and consistently simply is.

It is here, in the cup of coffee on the desk. It is these words, these thoughts. There is nothing I can do to get this. This can't be got. This isn't the result of anything. Being doesn't happen because I do this or that. It happens regardless of what I do. It is the only constant.

I don't have this, no one does. Being cannot be possessed. It cannot be known even. It can only be. So, so simple. So, so beautiful.

23rd January 2011

Hmm. There appears to be an individual here who does not want to be here. The dance of being continues. Waking from the dream of separation seems to happen and then I go to sleep again when the individual returns. This is the worst place in the world to be. Caught between two worlds.

When the sense of self returns it comes very powerfully with a desire to end self. The self now seeks its own demise and looks for ways to bring it about. Of course, that cannot occur. The whole time there is a self trying to get rid of a self, there is a big brute of a self doing he getting rid of!

I think I'll just go and make a cup of tea and sit and listen to some music.

26th January 2011

The most fascinating thing that is happening here tonight is that I cannot find 'me'. If I look with any real attention, I do not find this thing called me. All that is here are experiences. If I close my eyes and take a moment to look inside, all I see are things happening. Emotions, thoughts, physical sensations in the body, sounds, smells.

The thoughts and feelings that are happening are sometimes very powerful and it feels very much like they are happening to me. There is an entity here, a separate person that all of those things happen to. I am anxious or angry or frustrated or worried or I am happy or excited or stimulated or relaxed or at peace. It's all happening to me. I own it. It's my experience and I'm responsible for it.

Yet… where is this me that owns all of that? It seems that I am located within this body. But where? Me is obviously not just a physical organism. Mostly, me is the thoughts and emotions that make up my experience. But where is this me? One can look and look and this me will never be found. All that will be found are experiences, all that will be found is whatever is happening here and now.

The only thing that is certain is that this is always this. This is never not this, whatever this is. There is only this. And this is simply being whatever this is, in all its glorious differentiated manifestation.

This is always this.

31st January 2011

Well, what a month! I feel like I've lived a lifetime in 31 days. I've been feeling for a while like things are collapsing and at times it's been quite unsettling. So much of this awakening reminds me of times when I've fallen apart mentally and emotionally in the past that there are times when I wonder if that is what is really going on.

There has been a great amount of change in the past few months. The story of me, the story of my life situation is quite chaotic and that obviously throws up some challenges, especially when there is a sense of a self that it's all happening to. When it feels like my life is falling apart, it gets scary.

And then there are the moments when it's seen there is no one who has a life, there is just stuff happening. No one has a life so no one's life can fall apart! And certainly the story of me doesn't seem to have quite the same pulling power as before. This story doesn't sell as many tickets as it once did.

There is more and more a letting go almost. A tense feeling may arise for example and the instinct now is to immediately relax into it. There is less drama with feelings of anxiety or feelings of fear. There is a great deal of pressure to find some kind of regular work now, a way to support myself and pay for essentials.

If what is happening is 'being out of work', then 'looking for a job' happens. Or it doesn't. Either way, it's not a problem. It's just what is happening.

2nd February 2011

There is absolutely nothing on offer for a person in non-duality. Promises can be made and sometimes are made. You might be told that you can abide in non-dual awareness, that you can have peace, contentment or that you can become free from the complexity and pain of being a person.

All of that is still very dual. Who is going to become free? Who is going to get peace? This is still two. A person and the peace or freedom the person gets. And who is going to abide in non-dual awareness? When there is no person there owning everything, there is only non-dual awareness. There is no need for anyone to do anything to get it or to be in it.

As seekers, we desperately want to have something to look forward to. We want someone (a guru perhaps) to make promises to us. It's safe, it's what's expected, it's what we came here for.

And when we are promised an experience or a path toward change that will finally fix our complicated life, we feel comforted, we feel we still have choice and control.

There is no choice, no control and no path or system or practice is going to deliver all of the goodies that seem to be on offer. Whatever is offered at the spiritual buffet can be taken away in minutes when life threatens whatever it is we think we've found. That does not mean stop seeking and put away your meditation cushion. I'm not interested in telling anyone what to do. There is no one who can do anything anyway, so who is going to stop seeking?

Knowing and understanding that there is no one here who can seek or not seek does not of course stop us seeking. Still we look for a way out. How can I dissolve this seeking self? What can I do? There really is nothing you or I can do. There is nothing we need to do. Life is already whole and complete. Our seeking is not separate from that wholeness. It is that wholeness.

And yet, we desperately want to experience that wholeness. We want to own it, we want it to happen to us. It will never happen. It will never happen, because there is only wholeness and the seeking and the wanting to own wholeness is wholeness too.

3rd February 2011

What is happening? Body is bodying, room is rooming, pen is writing, thoughts are thinking, ears are listening, eyes are seeing, Michael is Michael-ling, birds are tweeting, clouds are moving, wind is rustling in the trees.

When there is just life happening, when there is no one owning this life, life unfolds with infinitely more ease.

8th February 2011

Life flows. Regardless of what I do or don't do, life flows. It may flow gently, it may meander, it may flow in rapid torrents, but flow it does. Life lives, whether I believe I am living it or not.

When I am not in the way of life flowing, when there is no separate self taking ownership of life flowing there is inevitably less struggle. There may be pain or difficulty or anger or anxiety but there is only that. There is no me separate from it, whatever it happens to be.

At the moment, all there is, is sitting on a chair, writing in a notebook, breathing. It is safe and calm and easy. It might just as well be panic or worry or planning or working. But it is only ever that. Freely this, radically alive... whirling, sparkling, scudding, shooting, scooting.

11th February 2011

It's amazing how the various messages that we see in the world of non-duality have always been with us through art, music, poetry, theatre and of course many of the traditional spiritual and religious texts. Hidden and overlooked for the most part. I can certainly say that since encountering the Open Secret message from Tony Parsons (and the writing/speaking of others) I seem to be spotting the infinite winking at me everywhere.

The other evening I was listening to a k.d lang album that I'd not heard properly for about 15 years. On it, there is a song called 'Infinite and Unforeseen'. In this post I'm going to interpret the main lyric from a non-dual perspective (if there is such a thing!)

Here's the main lyric I'm going to focus on:
It takes you by surprise
There before your eyes
A place you've always been

A place you've always been
Infinite and unforeseen

"It takes you by surprise." How true is that? A clear seeing of
Being is a complete surprise, whether you've been specifically
seeking that seeing or not. This is a love song and falling in love is
always a complete surprise. You can't plan to fall in love, you
can't schedule it. It either happens or not. And when this is seen,
when being is seen it is like falling in love. It's a total surprise!"

There before your eyes". Exactly! One of the things that is so
surprising about seeing this is that it's right where you are, right in
front of you... it's this! You don't have to go anywhere, you don't
have to do anything, it's being done before your very eyes!

"A place you've always been". Being is never not being. This is
never not this, has never not been this. It's pointing to the one
constant: being. You've never not been here!

"Infinite and unforeseen". This is the infinite and it is unforeseen,
because when there is a seeing, it happens when there is no one
there looking. Stunning, beautiful... art has a way of delivering
this message in such an uncluttered way, it's amazing.

Messages of non-duality and even blogging about it can sometimes
take being and make it very sterile and intellectual. I find that
music or art can cut through the tendency for the mind to wrangle
with it in a way that discussion alone cannot. This is a LOVE affair
with life, in all of its glory and it's horror.

15th February 2011

Am sat in the cafe in the square, feeling nerves rise. Anxiety is
happening. The separate self feels threatened by something.

This is being also. This, the pen, the chatter in the coffee shop, the
music, the table, the chair, the heart pumping, the thoughts

arriving, the breath, the sound, the silence the sound spills out of.. it's all being, being this.

Breathe.

The story of me is compelling only to me and possibly to other me's. It's just a story. What is actually happening? Blood is coursing through the veins, heart is pumping, tummy is turning over, thoughts are tumbling over in the mind... it's all being, being that. Nothing is threatened. Being cannot threaten itself. What is happening is being.. being is being anxiety and being the feeling that a separate self is threatened.

There is nothing outside of being, so nothing can threaten it. It all happens and un-happens here.

16th February 2011

In liberation, we are left nowhere, with nothing, knowing nothing. This is a terrible dilemma for the individual. The thought of being left with nothing throws up lots of emotion for most of us. Fear, sadness, anger, frustration. To the individual, nothing is a bad thing. A void, emptiness, bankruptcy. Ultimately, it signifies death. It symbolises the end of me and so naturally, me does not like that idea.

The individual doesn't usually know this, but whenever it desires something it is the absence of itself that it truly craves. And so, the individual does not like what it thinks is nothing but nothing is the answer is so desperately seeks.

Knowing nothing. There are two ways of interpreting those words. The first (and the most common) sees those words as a bad thing. Who wants to know nothing? What value could that possibly have? Well to the seeker, none at all. And in a world that values lots of 'somethings', knowing nothing won't secure you a good deal. And as seekers, that is what we want.

The other way of interpreting those words cannot be easily explained. It requires an all together different seeing. And it's not a case of simply deciding to look at it from another angle. It is really seeing that nothing is not only a blank void. Not only emptiness, but that it is it's opposite. Nothing is everything. Emptiness is fullness. The formless is form.

Knowing nothing can then be a celebration. When you know nothing, you know everything. One could say that when you are left with nothing, you have riches beyond description... riches that can never be taken away. But of course, you don't have those riches... you ARE those riches.

And that might be the most confrontational message of all. Not only are you left with nothing, not only do you know nothing, you are nothing. To the individual, that's bad news. To you, it's cause for great celebration!

19th February 2011

The hardest thing for the self to accept when it comes to considering this freedom is that it is all inclusive. Which means the good and the bad are free to be. Those things that I might wish to be free from can still occur. Impatience, anxiety, fear, doubt, anger, sadness, boredom, restlessness, irritation all happen in freedom. It does not exclude anything.

The separate self simply cannot let go of the idea that freedom means feeling good all the time, feeling floaty and high and nice and fluffy.

Freedom is not the end of anything but the sense that I am separate from life. When there is no one here living this life, it is the end of conflict with whatever happens. There simply is no one to argue with anxiety or fear or anger, there is no one to insist it should not be happening.

23rd February 2011

There is a very clear feeling of freshness happening tonight. Very alive and very ordinary. Quite a free feeling, unspectacular in a way. But from the point of view of the individual, it is spectacular and worth reporting. The individual thinks it's found some treasure. It's a light feeling, a feeling of lightness in the body. Everything feels right. Certainly a feeling of being at home or as I used to hear people say years ago, feeling at one with myself. Of course, there is no self to be at one with but I get a sense that phrase is trying to point to the simple such-ness of being. A very natural and very common-place feeling of oneness.

We all feel this from time to time. It's a feeling of being at home. So markedly different from the low level tension of always feeling slightly out of place or as though something unidentifiable is missing. So different in quality from that feeling of lack, that feeling of hunger. And when this happens, when all there is, is this, it is realised that there is no quantum leap that takes place. It seems that way, but in reality it's a small step really. Here is no great distance away! It's here! And without any effort to be here, it can suddenly be realised that here is all there is. And out of that comes a feeling of wholeness, a feeling that one has come home.

There is really nothing you can do to get this. Because it's not something you have, not something you can pick up and hold and take home. It is home. It's not a trinket from a fair. I don't have anything distinct, I have no object. It is a being. It is being, simply being itself without the layer of me. It is naked being, without the clothing of me. Totally alive, totally fresh and with it comes a sort of natural vulnerability. So, it's slightly risky. Very open. A childlike openness to the world. A sort of wonder. A simple yet very profound sense of wonder and awe.

And it's not the kind of awe we imagine one might have for God or angels or beings of light. It's simpler than that, much more ordinary than that. And yet it has this power about it. It's humming and throbbing with aliveness. A very clear, very open feeling. A feeling in fact of being totally empty. Totally empty of self and full of everything else. Full with this moment and everything appearing in awareness but totally absent… no one there to experience it, no individual interpreting. No self measuring and judging. No me, but everything else.

There is also a very strong sense that this is given freely too. It's not the result of anything. No work produces this. It's not the maturing of any investment. No effort can produce this. It's totally and freely given. No matter what mess you are in, no matter how bad or good you've been, this is freely given. You can't earn this by doing good deeds. This is not a prize you win when you insert a coin.

It's not a place you visit either. It's always here. It is the space of all location. It is location-less. It seems to the individual that this is a place that can be visited from time to time, but no. This is always the case. It is the individual who comes and goes and we mistake that for being coming and going. Being never comes and never goes anywhere. Being always is.

And that is felt when there is no me getting in the way. It is not felt by you or me, but by being itself.

25th February 2011

Seeking is all about coming home. All seeking is a search to return home, to feel at home.

Home is wholeness, is oneness. Home is the paradise we thought we lost. This is home.

Home is what is happening. Home is being, happening. You are being, you are home. You are not at home, for there is no you to be at home. You are home itself.

There is nothing but home. Home is all there is. Home is what you are.

So, put your feet up!

2nd March 2011

Thoughts are happening but no one is really listening. It's like there are teenagers upstairs playing loud music but there is no one in to tell them to be quiet!

Sometimes there is an ability to communicate here and sometimes not. Today and tonight it's been a bit scattered. Again and again there is the instinct to let go. The thought that I should do this or that arises and either I do or I don't.

Language cannot describe this. It can attempt to but it will always fail. Sometimes it's possible to capture the flavour of it but it can't ever pin it down. It is eternity and eternity has no edges, no beginning or end. There are no boundaries so you can't stick it in a book or frame and put it on the wall.

It seems some kind of weaning back into being is happening. It feels like a process but it's certainly not one that can be measured. Being is timeless and glimpses or awakenings happen in timelessness so there is no way to measure any kind of progress. It's not a ten part course.

5th March 2011

There is really no way to talk about non-duality, about liberation, about freedom. Whatever we say about it, is not it. The finger pointing at the moon is not the moon, the map is not the territory.

And yet, the words come. This is emptiness writing, silence sounding, stillness moving. Sometimes, a hint of the flavour of this might be heard. What can seem to happen is the boundlessness that is pointed to can resonate with the boundlessness that you are, deep calls to deep as it were and in that, the separate sense of self can slip away.

The separate self of course wants to know what that is like. There have been many times when I've longed to know what it's like to experience liberation. But whenever it is seen, it is seen that no one experiences it. It simply is, without anyone knowing it or experiencing it. That sounds like it might be a trip or a weird psychedelic happening and yet it's totally ordinary.

Life as it is, is seen without the layer of me. So, it's the most sober and gentle kind of trip really! Everything does tend to take on a new kind of depth but nothing changes shape or colour and no one freaks out when 'me' slips away! Who could? There is no one there!

So, life is still life… the dishes still get washed, meals are cooked, the laundry gets done but there is no one who does it… and that is life, but not as we know it!

And so, this message is not all that interesting to a 'me'. You can't get anything from this and so it's often ignored or rejected. The message has been with us for many years. Jesus said you had to lose yourself to find yourself, a total paradox of course.

This is life lived in paradox. This is nothing being everything, totally empty and totally full.

Totally amazing, for no one.

8th March 2011

What is there left to see? Is there a me there, trying to get something? Do I write in this diary and on the blog to get freedom? What is the truth? Who is asking? Who wants to know?

If there is any doubt about liberation, liberation has not happened. When there is no one there, it's very obvious. So, the dance of self and no self stutters on. As Tony Parsons says, it's a dance of 'me-ing and being'.

9th March 2011

Somebody asked me this today.

"If there is nothing and there is no one… well… that can be quite depressing. And there's nothing in what you're saying to offer any help, so why not just jump off a cliff?"

Depression or despair can be one of the responses to this. The self cannot see the everything in the nothing, so it tries to picture its own idea of nothingness and what it tends to find is a blank void that seems terrifying, depressing or full of deep despair. The separate self fears its own absence the most and yet it is its own absence that it longs for.

So, the self is in a fix that it can't get out of. It truly is a catch 22 situation, until it isn't. That there is only this, that there is only nothing being everything can be seen by no one. But no one of course can make that happen. It's a total paradox that is never understood at all.

This you that you fear losing so much, can it actually be found? Close your eyes and see if you can find this thing called you? What do you find when you look inside? Feelings? Thoughts? Bodily sensations? Hearing, feeling, sounds, smells? Instinctively you know that none of it is you, none of it is who you are. Thoughts, not you. Feelings, not you. Sensations, not you. A body, not you.

Can you find what feels? What is thinking? What is aware of feelings? What is aware of thoughts?

All you actually find is silence. Is stillness. That is the nothing that you are. That nothing is totally full, it's totally alive. It's bristling with aliveness. This is not about a love affair with deadness. It's a total love affair with life, with being, with being alive.

So, the separate self wants help. Wants to feel better, to feel soothed. Yet, what it longs for it also fears. It longs for this, for the stillness and silence of nothing being everything yet it cannot bear to picture that without owning it and experiencing it.

12th March 2011

Everything about me and my life is so complicated. Every me and it's story is so complex. But being is so joyfully uncomplicated.

When nothing but this is happening, it's amazing. The wonder and joy is indescribable. It's very ordinary, it's very simple and yet very powerful. Beautiful. It's very alive. The sound of the music, the light in the room, the buzzing of the fridge, the leaping of thoughts, the fluttering of feelings.

16th March 2011

We are all dying to live really. In the sense that we are desperate to live, impatient to live.

All of our seeking is focused toward living more fully. To have more, see more, know more, do more, be more. We yearn to be more fully satisfied, to be finally fulfilled.

We do not see that true fulfilment is only found when seeking ends. When we stop looking here, there and everywhere for what we think might fix us, then the sheer fullness of this is seen and it is enough.

The problem for a separate seeker however is that it cannot stem it's need and compulsion to seek. So, while the end of seeking is actually what is sought, no seeker and no seeking can bring that about.

No amount of seeking can end seeking.

What can happen when the pure being that we are is pointed to, is an energetic resonance that can seem to dissolve the sense of separation.

Nothing really happens, because there is only being and the separate self is simply being, being a separate self. So any happening is only apparent.

What arises in this timeless being is the thought, experience and belief that there is such a thing called 'me' that is separate from timeless being.

That thought, experience and belief (and story) we call me can fall away and then there is only timeless being. And that is liberation. That is what we search for.

That is truly dying to live. The separate self dies and life lives anyway. Lives full on, passionately, total raw life, for no one.

And so nothing is offered here, apart from the possibility of death. Dying to live.

27th March 2011

I feel physically drained. I think I've got a cold. I should eat something but have no appetite.

Just watching the mind this morning has been quite entertaining. Thoughts are zinging all over the place. Mostly there is a dialogue about how bad things are, about how out of control my life is. Thoughts jump from one topic to another. One moment there are thoughts about the need to earn money the next moment there is a thought about how awakening is happening, then a thought that nothing needs to be done at all.

And then there might be a moment when the thoughts are zinging away but they seem part of wholeness, they are suddenly included in this completeness. And soon enough, the thoughts spin out into nothing and there is just this happening; doing the washing up, drinking coffee, listening to music, sitting on the sofa, writing in the diary.

30th March 2011

That which we are seeking, that which we long for, that which we fight wars for and wish for and look the world over for, is this. Is the being that is all things.

This being is all there is. It is everything. It is the being within all things. The timeless, dimensionless, still, silent, motionless, deathless nothing-ness is this, is being and it is what we seek.

It needn't be sought after, for you are it. All looking for it, overlooks that which is doing the looking. That which looks is what is looked for. That which searches is what is sought. It is all there is. There can be nothing else, there is nothing else. This is all and everything.

1st April 2011

At the moment there seems to be some confusion about how to make my life work mixed up with some clear moments of seeing there is no one who has a life, no one who owns a life to make it work or not.

I've been writing the blog for nearly a year now and sharing this dance of me-ing and being. Sometimes there is a complicated me here who has all the usual dramas about how to have more pleasure and avoid any pain and sometimes there is just the clear, uncluttered space of being itself.

I'm starting to wonder if this dance will ever end. Will this oscillating go on till the day I die?

YES!

Until the death of me, me will continue the game of being a better me. Me will want more pleasure, more stability, less pain, more money, more freedom, less struggle, less discomfort.

When the me dies, there is just the radical aliveness of life living.

2nd April 2011

The absence of the individual, the end of seeking, wholeness, oneness, being, life, freedom (call it what you like) is radically alive. It's raucous!

Alive, alive-O! Being, being alive. Outrageously alive, radically alive, robustly, abundantly… richly….

Life without me is when the greatest fun happens!

Life without the separate sense of self is a very rich aliveness, a very full, a very radical aliveness. It's radically alive, robustly and passionately and fully alive. It's a torrid love affair with living… at the same time gentle, soft, silent, pure, still and also radiantly and raucously alive and kicking.

It's a total in-love-ness with this. Without the effort, without the strain and stress of seeking, of striving, of rabidly hunting for final fulfilment, life simply is, simply happens in all its raw glory.

It is the brashness of blood shooting through veins, the explosion of one thought after another, the blossoming of feeling in the body, the fleshy is-ness of life. Bountiful, plentiful, richly diverse and flourishing. It is florid in its multiplicity, bursting with the sweet is-ness of life.

This is life, full on! Lived by no one! A miracle.

6th April 2011

Thoughts happen. One of the thoughts I had just now was that I must not be awakening, liberation has not happened here because my life is such a mess. So, the thought is that I must be doing something wrong. Surely, the thought goes, if I were liberated, my life would be a success?

The me simply will not let go of this notion that freedom means a successful life. The fact is, life is always successfully this! This is utter success here. Life is successfully being me, sat on the sofa, writing in my diary and wondering if liberation means a neat and tidy life.

Seeing this, there is no failure. Life cannot possibly fail to be fully alive in whatever way it shows up right now.

9th April 2011

I don't practice any kind of religion any more (and was never a real success at that to begin with) and I've never been at home with a lot of religious language. I especially avoid using words like God or Spirit at the moment as I find their associations can create a great deal of confusion.

If I do use the word God these days, it's to point to this, to being, to oneness, wholeness, liberation. It's certainly not the God I grew up believing (and sometimes not believing) in. And I find that God is not a useful pointer to this.

But, it's worth saying that any idea of God is this too. Is being, being our ideas of God. It's the same as being showing up as suffering, or pencils, or snot or a nuclear bomb.

A few years back, this phrase found its way into my head: "This is just another way for you to be with me".

And I got a strong sense that if God were to speak to me at that moment, that is what he would have said.

This is just another way for you to be with me. That phrase came back to me tonight as I was messaging with someone. And it seems appropriate now to revisit it.

This total intimacy with life is not one being with another, however. Wholeness being totally whole simply cannot be described. But it's turn of phrase that might resonate however, so I thought I'd share it.

God is saying, life is saying, being is saying, nothing is saying:

This is just another way for you to be with me.

Eventually, the idea that I am someone who can be with a God falls away. In the end, what is perhaps heard is that any experience, any thought, any sensation, any appearance is just another way love is.

Unconditional love simply is everything. Nothing is left out. All the pain, all the crap, all the glory, all the softness, all the screeching, the yearning, the seeking, searching, longing, hunting, forgiving, resting, living, the singing, the forgetting, the getting and the giving…

This is just another way for love to be. Love is being you, in all ways.

12th April 2011

What is this miracle? This spectacular display of ordinary being? It is a festival of aliveness, this explosion of colour and sound, this breathtaking display. A pageant, a carnival of diverse multiplicity, an amazing, indescribable and beautiful spectacle! This great concert of life! A rich and colourful feast, a great banquet of aliveness.

Just the very here-ness of now is so fucking amazing! Vital life, vibrant and pulsating, throbbing with presence, humming with aliveness. Something amazing is happening. Every second a miracle is happening. The constant miracle, the miracle of being, the miracle of life. Effortless unfolding, unspeakable beauty.

I stand aghast at the sheer, utter wonder of it all. Sheer, utter joy in the very is-ness of this. The very is of it.

Of course, the individual wants to do something with this. It attempts to objectify it, to turn this no-thing-ness into a thing, into something distinct and discreet. It would like this to be some special power, some special place or experience. Something holy to be worshiped or something to be used to great advantage.

This is stillness moving. This is paradise, right here.

17th April 2011

A lot of people on the spiritual search will inevitably come across meditation or other practices. For a few years, I tried to develop practices and often failed. Failed in the sense that I rarely found a practice that I could repeat and enjoy or (as is more often the case for many people) I failed to find something that 'worked' for me.

What does that mean, exactly? It means that I was engaging in practice for the specific purpose of getting something out of it. I would meditate or pray or self enquire or do shadow work with the express purpose of getting some spiritual rewards. It was all part and parcel of the quest for enlightenment, which set off from the premise that there was something wrong with ' me', that I was un-enlightened, damaged or broken and needed to wake up, to be fixed or saved.

It is from this position of not enough that many of us begin a spiritual practice. It is, for many, the whole reason that the idea of practice appears and seems attractive.

And sometimes, I did seem to benefit from my practices. I might have felt happier for a time, may have had some insights, found clarity or a calm mind. My life certainly seemed less obviously and outwardly chaotic.

There is nothing right or wrong with practice. It's important to say that being is being this whether it's being addictive patterns or whether it's being you meditating. Practices like meditation or self enquiry or shadow work or personal development can make a difference to the dream of separation. It can make the dream more comfortable, for a while.

To someone who is suffering from physical ill health, mental turmoil, grief, addiction, emotional distress, depression and so on, I would say that a practice such as meditation can certainly bring some relief. It may well make your dream story more bearable, enjoyable even.

If meditation or prayer improves your physical health, it certainly has some relative value. Of course.

What I found was that although there was less chaos and drama outwardly in my life, a new kind of chaos was found. An existential chaos began to take place!

So, it is generally found that any relief or relaxation or enjoyment or improvement of the story is discovered eventually to be temporary. The dysfunction we may experience is a symptom of separation, a symptom of the dream story and so while the dream story can be improved by practices, the dreamer is still dreaming. And that seems to eventually cause an unease, a sense of dissatisfaction, of disquiet and can easily grow into despair.

It is found that whatever improvement is made to the story, was not, after all, the final answer. But that is not to say that improvements to the story are not valuable. Again, relatively speaking, they certainly seem to be for many people.

Though, it's also observable that there are many more for whom spiritual practice just doesn't fill the hole. We still feel incomplete.

Meditation for me is very much about resting in and as awareness, resting in and as being. When there is no separation, when the dream is over, when there is no sense of being a separate self, resting in and as being, in and as awareness is your natural way of existing. In that sense, every experience is a meditation.

There is no longer any need to sit with eyes closed. Walking to work is a meditation, eating your breakfast is a meditation, speaking, listening to music, writing, drinking red wine, laughing, crying. It's all being, it's all awareness showing up as that.

So, should we meditate? It's entirely a personal choice, in the end. When resting in and as awareness is not a means to end but an end in itself, it can indeed be a very pleasurable non-activity.

When there is no one doing this or that, when life is not happening to anyone, it is seen that many of life's activities are pleasurable, contain deep joy and infinite depth.

And because nothing is excluded in being, sadness or anger or boredom may arise, but they arise for no one, they happen to no one, so they have their own unique beauty, in that they are freely and rawly what is.

So, meditation can seem to help improve the dream story. Or it may not. Either way, the whole time there is someone who meditates, someone who does meditation, the dream story continues. I am meditating or meditation is happening to me, is the story.

When there is no one doing meditation, mediation happens much the same way doing the washing up happens or cooking the dinner. Because of that, a special time to sit and practice tends to fall away as it's no longer relied upon to complete 'me'.

I often sit still, in silence. But I don't do it for any purpose. There is no agenda in sitting quietly. It is just what's happening.

21st April 2011

Totally unconditional love allows everything, even the darkness. In its embrace, all dualities become one. It is impossible to understand with the mind.

It is gloriously simple. Everything is this, there is nothing that is not. All the muck and the goo, all the boredom and the anger and the irritation and the doubt, all the glory and the horror, the joy and the beauty, the confusion and the clarity, it's all this.

There is no escape... love will never let you go.

25th April 2011

Talking about this really is trying to catch water in a net. And yet, the trying to talk about, the net and the water (and my computer, the fingers typing, the words appearing) are also it.

This never, ever leaves you. It never leaves you, it goes everywhere with you because you ARE it. It is the simplest homecoming ever. The homecoming that never really happens, because you never left in the first place.

Liberation is the end of something that was never happening. That which was never happening was the belief that you'd left home in the first place. You never did. You can never leave home, because home is what you ARE.

You can never reach enlightenment. The effort to reach enlightenment just keeps you separate from that which you are. Enlightenment is not something you reach, because enlightenment is what you ARE.

You ARE this. And when you are, you 'be'. You are 'are-ing' ... you are being! You are it!

28th April 2011

The sense of me desperately wants something spectacular. It wants a special event, a special experience. It thinks that liberation is the most special and spectacular thing that can happen. It imagines that liberation will make it special and important.

It imagines that liberation will make everything better, that it will fix me. It thinks liberation is some kind of magic pill or potion that will cure all the ills of my life. It thinks that taking this potion will make me permanently happy.

The freedom of liberation includes all that perceived illness. All that perceived bad stuff. And yet it is also beyond it. It is beyond it because in liberation the illness is seen to be both real and unreal. No longer is there just something happening but there is nothing being something happening. It's quite different.

The me clings to the idea that liberation will heal me. It won't. It will destroy me. It will reveal the me to be a mirage, simply an appearance here. A slight deception.

The me may want to die, to burst like a soap bubble but it insists on being there to witness it. The me wants to die with one eye open.

30th April 2011

Emotions are arising. Feelings in the body. A sense of restlessness. The feeling that perhaps I should be doing something. A kind of boredom, a kind of irritation? It's difficult to find a name for it without a story that goes with it.

One of the things I used to believe about liberation is that once it happens, there will be no more negative experiences. Why else would we call it liberation? The funny thing is, in liberation so called negative emotions or experiences can still happen. Do still happen. But no one is saying they should not be there. There is no one telling a story about the experiences or feelings, there is no one pushing them away. So, in that sense they are no longer labelled as negative. They are simply what they are, totally what they are.

Restlessness is totally and wholly restlessness. It is freely restlessness, with no one judging it, owning it, making it in to an identity, pushing it away or telling a story about it. Then there is no such thing as negative experience, there is just experience.

Jeff Foster has a nice way of saying it. That there is freedom IN whatever arises. Freedom within the so called negative experiences or emotion. This is radical freedom. The freedom that allows both pain and pleasure, sadness and happiness.

So, there is a sense of restlessness here today. The miraculous thing about it is, these feelings are just happening in empty space. It's not really happening to me. There is no one here who is saying that those feeling shouldn't be here. They are here and their very presence IS their acceptance. The moment they arise, they are accepted. Because they arise, they are accepted. There is no one doing the acceptance. It just is. Life is the acceptance. The feelings arising are life arising as the feeling of restlessness and life is the space in which they are accepted.

Amazing.

2nd May 2011

I dreamt I was writing another blog post last night. That happens a lot at the moment. It's like I'm writing in my sleep, but aware enough to construct whole sentences and paragraphs and remember them when I wake up.

There is nothing you can do or think or feel that is not this. There is nowhere you can go that is not here. You cannot not be this, you cannot not be here and this cannot not be now. You are this, here now.

Wherever you go, whatever you do, whatever you think or feel, this is it. Paradise is always happening. It's not a place or a destination. It is the being that is happening. It is eternity. In all its ghastly horror and all its miraculous splendour.

5th May 2011

Everything that can be seen and touched and tasted and smelt and heard and sensed here is an appearance. Even thought appears in you. Thoughts are much like the flowers and the trees and the tea cups and the planes flying by. They all appear here, they all appear within you.

Adyashanti has a lovely way to say it: even you appear in you. The sense of self we come to know as 'me' appears here, appears in you. You are the screen on which the movie of your life plays out. Plays out as you.

Such joyous freedom in that. The movement away from wholeness, the movement toward it, is already it. Totally inescapable.

There is nowhere for the mind to land, no foothold. No concept is clear enough to express this, no clarity of ideas or understanding will ever be this.

Knowing about this and being this are so different. When there is no one looking, suddenly, everything is a pointing to this.

7th May 2011

Spain

We're in Spain for a long weekend. It's lovely to be somewhere different and enjoy the warm weather. The view of the sky and the sea from the balcony of the apartment is beautiful and there are lots of swallows diving and swooping by the window.

Sitting here and looking out at the vastness of the sky is such a wonder! It's almost as if the vastness that I am is singing with the vastness of the sky and celebrating in the swooping of the swallows and the smudges of pastel pinks and fluffy whites in the clouds.

Being is so gentle, so beautiful, so startling and so total. The strongest embrace, the softest touch. Indescribable.

11th May 2011

Many non-dual writers and speakers have pointed to the total intimacy in this seeing. What is this seeing, what do I mean by that? It's really seeing no separation. It's the end of the belief and experience of being a separate part of the whole. It is being the whole, seeing the whole in everything and everywhere. Being the whole, seeing itself everywhere. And so everything is totally intimate. There is nothing outside of this.

What I notice more and more these days is that utter intimacy. I frequently sit on the sofa in my kitchen, simply sitting. Usually, the only sounds I can hear is the clock ticking and every now and then the gurgling of the fridge. What I notice more and more is that I cannot find where the ticking clock ends and I begin. There is the sound and the sound appears here, in my awareness. Even my awareness occurs here. In that sense, nothing is ever outside of me.

I can see how that might sound like a strange or unusual experience. But it has such a natural feel to it. A sense of ease that I vaguely remember from childhood. This intimacy is very ordinary and brings with it a natural acceptance of what is. Even the simplest of things take on a new depth. Walking from one room to another has never happened before, it's happening for the first time and is stunning! It's the wonder of a child at seeing this for the very first time.

Take a moment to look around you, listen to the sounds, let the senses drink it all in. Can you find the point where you end and all that you see and sense, begins? Doesn't the world you see and 'you' arise and fall away together, totally and intimately as one?

14ᵗʰ May 2011

I am sat in the garden. It's just before 9pm. The sun is setting on the other side of the house, there is a slight chill in the air.

I look around me, my senses drinking in the scene. It is suddenly (and paradoxically) clear that there is no way I can know what this is.

I can smell earth. I hear the sounds of two wood pigeons cooing in the trees (or are they on the roof?), the sound of a television burbling out of a the neighbours open window, birds are cheeping, the distant sound of traffic, the drone of an airplane engine, a child running up a path.

I see the tree at the end of the garden. I know of course that what I am looking at is a tree and yet, at the same time, I do not know what it is. Tree somehow does not capture the mystery of this sensory experience. All I find in 'tree' is a collection of concepts about this experience. Associations I have about trees, about this tree, thoughts I have handed to me by literature, my culture, my personal history and memories. Nowhere in those concepts do I find *this*. This vibrantly alive happening.

Seeing in this way feels like seeing through the eyes of a child that has not yet learned language and concepts, a child that has not yet begun to label and categorise the world and the sensory experiences offered. It's a raw, feet first kind of seeing. And yet, as what is seen is both unknown and at the same time known, the advantages of conceptualised seeing are not lost.

For the purposes of functioning within society I can instantly call upon all the shared concepts to communicate about the tree as well as drawing upon my own emotional, creative and intellectual interpretations of the tree.

And still, there is the unspeakable wonder of what is happening. The sheer delight in not knowing. There is an innocence and vulnerability in this seeing. It is being reborn and seeing this mystery afresh. All that is known about 'tree' can be set aside, always available should I need those concepts.

For now, the joy is in suddenly not knowing what this is. I do not know, I do not know... and it's beautiful, it's thrilling.

1st June 2011

Feel very alive tonight. There is such joy in simply being. Such joy in sitting, in the gurgling of the fridge, in the ticking of the clock, in the movement of the pen across the page.

Met up with a friend for a drink earlier. He's going through a divorce with his wife at the moment and there is a lot of uncertainty as it's in the early stages. We chatted and I listened mostly. It's funny, but there is no compulsion to explain this nondual seeing in situations like that. It's enough to just be.

There is no interest in signing anyone up to this, no pull to convert anyone. Being is being this in every form, in every way so there is no thought that anything could possibly not already be this freedom. In that sense, there is no need to evangelise or promote this. How do you promote what is? It already is and needs no promoting.

18th June 2011

This love is so gentle and so amazingly powerful. It's magnificent in it's simply humility. Being everything, it needs nothing. It does not want, it simply is. Sheer, unbounded joy!

Gently shattering all concepts of this, quietly and lovingly burning up all images of this in the fire of now, the fire of life.

All that is left is silence. Only the beautiful song of the world.

22nd June 2011

What's in it for me? What will I get? How will it make me feel? What kind of benefits will I receive?

In liberation nothing is held onto, so you don't get to keep anything. You don't draw any lasting benefit from this. It doesn't provide any improvement to the story of me, yet the story is allowed to continue, does continue.

So, all the good stuff still happens... as does the so called bad stuff.... you just don't own any of it. It's not yours to keep. You don't get to hold onto the good stuff anymore (you never did anyway) but also, there is no longer any holding onto the bad stuff.

The appearances of life are free to come and go. Like they always have been.

There is really no more clinging to anything. No clinging to people, to ideas, to experiences, to hopes, dreams, fears, emotions, thoughts, images of yourself or others, good or bad... no clinging to life because it's seen that you are life. You don't need to cling to what you are.

When you cling to what you are, you create the illusion that you are somehow separate from what you are, separate from life. This is the illusion, the dream we long to awaken from.

How do you end an illusion? What happens when an illusion ends? In essence, nothing happens because what you thought was happening was an illusion... nothing was happening.

25th June 2011

Am sat in the bedroom with the late afternoon sun spilling through. It's so gracious, the sunlight. So utterly and simply itself. Totally uncomplicated and complete as it is.

Feelings breeze in and out, life breathes, moves, writes, eats, sleeps. It's not going anywhere, there is no purpose in it's being. This is its beauty and its wonder. All of this diversity, this festival of living for the sheer joy of it.

Seeing this is coming home. Coming home to who you really are. Being this, being that. It's the most powerful love in the universe. It IS the universe.

29th June 2011

This cannot be known in any sense of the mind knowing this. If there is any knowing of it, it is known through the being of it. So, on the one hand this is totally known because it is your natural way of being. On the other hand, it cannot be known in any intellectual sense, or understood by the mind or collected and owned in the way we might know facts and figures or the way we might know an object or a process.

There is a natural being of this, you are simply being this, being whole, complete, one, when the filter of 'me' is not operating. You could say that our default setting is to simply be but that through our interaction with our world, family and culture, our default settings get customised. Depending on where on the planet you grow up, who your parents are, what the culture is like, the environment, social, political influences and so on…all of this can determine how this natural way of being, this natural default setting gets customised… and all individuals have a unique character.

So, in that sense this way of being, simply being this is not mysterious because it is your natural setting.. your natural way of being. But we cannot know what it is or why it is. This of course is not questioned in young children whose natural way of being has not been dramatically altered by conditioning.. . it is only when we think we can approach this natural way of being, only when we imagine we can hold it up and examine it as a separate object that we seek to know it in that way.

There is much in life that is a total mystery yet totally familiar. So, this is the obvious mystery. It's a mystery because we don't know what it is or why it is but it is also totally obvious, because it is all there is. It's totally obvious and utterly familiar because it is what you are. It's hidden in plain view.

3rd July 2011

It's late and I'm feeling quite tired but I don't want to sleep just yet. This is-ness is so intoxicating, so delicious, so thrilling. I could almost just write anything to simply be here, to be present with the scratch-scratch of the pen on paper, the sound of the fridge gurgling, the feel of my feet in slippers.

I'm enjoying sharing my writing on the blog. I signed up to facebook and shared some of the posts through that. It's interesting to see what happens when different people read and respond. Lots of people have clearly enjoyed the expressions and some have sent some lovely messages. And there have been some people who are suspicious of my intentions in writing, questioning the authenticity of what is shared.

There is no sense of ownership over what is written so it's impossible to be offended by any rejection of what I'm sharing or of any harsh criticism. Being doesn't need me to write about it or even need to be seen at all. It simply and gloriously is this, whatever the weather.

So, people come and read the blog and some enjoy it and some criticise it. And the wind rustles the leaves on the tree in the garden and the clock is ticking and the fridge is doing that gurgling thing again.

9th July 2011

This doesn't need maintaining. You don't have to remember to be this, to be what you are. It simply naturally is, without the need for any effort.

In fact, the effort to be what you already are creates the illusion that you are not this. That you are separate and alone. And yet that illusion cannot escape the all inclusiveness of being.

Being is simply being the illusion.

So, being this actually happens regardless of whether you make effort or not. When you make an effort to be this, that is also being this. And what can arise in being this is the thought and belief that you are not being this.

That is how free this is, everything is allowed. How could being resist the temptation to pretend to not be this? And then discover, as if for the first time, that it is already being this even in its pretending not to be!

When the thought, belief and experience of being separate from this falls away, being this is all that is happening. It was all that was ever happening.

13th July 2011

Allergies are bad this morning. Eyes itching lots but no sneezing yet. It's definitely making me quite tired.

So, what is happening? What is showing up here? Is there irritation? A slight tightness? What is it, before I name it and categorise it? Movement, life energy moving through the body. Thoughts perhaps and feelings responding to the thoughts.

In truth, it's a total mystery and totally felt right here.

16th July 2011

Being stands out as this or that, stands out as you or me, as the flower, the buildings, the dog shit, the feeling of happiness and yet it is not separately any of these things. It is no one 'thing' alone. It is everything.

Being may stand out as the label 'being' or wholeness or consciousness or completeness and yet it is not simply the label, not simply the concept. Whatever being stands out as is a temporary expression of being.

One of the activities of mind is to analyse, to categorise, to know. It is really the owning impulse of the separate self. The separate self feels 'not enough' and so to compensate for that it goes out into the world and collects things, it accumulates all manner of things in order to comfort itself and one of the things it tries to accumulate is knowledge.

If I can know something, I can use that knowledge for my own gain, my protection or to achieve my goals. And that may work for building a house or launching a business. But when we take this approach with what some call liberation, we are doomed to failure. Try as we might, our understanding minds cannot grasp this, cannot work it out.

The beauty is that it needs no working out. All attempts to 'work it out' are it. You are what you seek. The end of seeking is the end of the illusion that you are separate and incomplete and need to find oneness or completion in the future. The end of an illusion the end of nothing. When the oasis is seen to be a mirage and there is only more desert, there is no event that takes place. There is no transformation. The illusion vanishes and so what was already happening (desert being more desert) is still happening as it already was, only now without the illusion of oasis.

This is the loss of something that was never owned in the first place, the loss of something that never existed in reality. It is the loss of the idea, belief and experience of separation. It is waking up in total poverty, owning nothing. And in owning nothing the richness of being is lived.

24th July 2011

There is the sense today that there is nothing to say in the face of this miraculous beauty, this stunning such-ness. Love in the very unfolding of this, showing up as the noise of this coffee shop, the sound of the couple behind me bickering, the steam on the windows, the heat of the day, the sun spilling over the table.

So, there is nothing to do but live.

27th July 2011

Many people hear that liberation or freedom is the end of seeking. That what we are actually looking for IS the end of seeking. Since you are what you seek, simply being what you are is the end of seeking. Seeking naturally ends when it is seen that you are already being that which you long for.

This does not mean that ALL desire stops! The desire for clean water, for nutritious food, for health, for sex, can and most likely will (thankfully!) still arise.

After all, what kind of paradise doesn't have decent food, good bars and plenty of healthy sex!?

Liberation is not the end of desire but the end of wanting the desired to set us free. What you want won't set you free. You are free already. What you want is simply an expression of that freedom.

Seeking is happening when you want XY or Z in order to set you free. So, all seeking begins from the assumption that you are not already free… that you can find freedom in the future. Seeking needs time, needs separation.

Liberation is the end of separation and that does not mean that there are no more appearances. It means that nothing that appears is separate. It's all this, including your desire for ice cream, or a healthy body, or a house by the sea.

In liberation it is simply seen that none of that will make you whole because you are whole already and all of that (desire) is included in that wholeness.

30th July 2011

Woke up this morning with a splitting headache. Drank a pint of water and sat for a bit in the kitchen. Watched the pain for a while at felt a kind of space around it. Then took a headache tablet.

Being gloriously shows up here as the headache, the pint of water, the practice of watching the pain and the headache tablet.

Life goes on being life, despite the story of awakening or the story of being un-awakened. In liberation there simply is no one to claim liberation or any kind of achievement. It's the end of any conflict with life, with what is.

There simply is the mystery of it all, for the sheer joy of it and the thrill that all of this happens and yet nothing happens at all. That is how forgiveness can happen, in seeing that no one needs forgiving because nothing happened at all.

There is this wonderful appearance, all the colour and light and sound. And you simply can't get any of it wrong. You can't get being alive wrong, you can't get being wrong. Such grace... such heartbreaking grace.

About the Author

Mike worked as an actor in London after studying at The Guildhall School of Music and Drama and later worked as a teacher and trainer. The feeling that something was missing in his life was ever present and like most people he constantly sought to make his life work better. At the age of 29 he was diagnosed with cancer and found himself facing death a lot earlier than anticipated. This experience kick started a voracious spiritual search. It was eventually seen that the spiritual search could only ever fail and in that failure, the utter success of this moment to be as it is was felt.

Mike began to write about the freedom that we are in a blog and to dialogue in conversations with others. Unlike previous spiritual experiences that came and went, the gentle and yet powerful simplicity of seeing reality without the filter of separation is ever present in the timeless unfolding of life as it is. It was seen that nothing needs to be added or taken away from this moment for freedom to shine.

Mike holds meetings in the UK where he shares pointers to the freedom that we are and also offers one to one sessions over Skype. You can read his regular blog and contact him online at

http://www.nothingsayingthis.com

CPSIA information can be obtained
at www.ICGtesting.com
Printed in the USA
LVOW13s1419120617
537827LV00037B/1534/P